Poems & Poetry

Robert M. Purcell

authorHOUSE®

It is an honor for me
to be able to give this to
comfort you

I hope you enjoy reading
it as much as I enjoyed
writing it

You have always been
special to me. This
is the way I can show it

Love you
Bobby

RM Purcell
(15 minute poet)

People near and dear   *by Robert M. Purcell*

Our love expressed

Experience that forms character

Music lyrics for a popular song

Stanzas to bring joy to those who reads them

& a collection that has inspired me

People in your life you can relate to

Our gratitude to friends

Experience talking you can use

Thanks to the people you love

Romantic philosophy on how to keep a woman

Yesterday's memories . . . tomorrows dreams . . .

AuthorHouse™
1663 Liberty Drive
Bloomington, IN 47403
www.authorhouse.com
Phone: 1-800-839-8640

First published by AuthorHouse   11/16/2011

ISBN: 978-1-4567-9906-9 (sc)
ISBN: 978-1-4567-9904-5 (hc)
ISBN: 978-1-4567-9902-1 (ebk)

Library of Congress Control Number: 2011917437

Printed in the United States of America

This book is printed on acid-free paper.

About the Book

This book contains the secrets to making
and keeping a
Woman, friends, relatives, people you do
Business with, feel appreciated

It gives a person a new way to
Look at life
Even when pain and illness strike

I give you a new way to look at poetry

Dedication

I will be dedicating this to my wife. After all,
without her there would be no poems at all

It is true she has put up with me and my illnesses.
She has put up with me losing my dad. She has
replaced him as the best friend I could ever have

She knows what it takes to make me break or bend.
My family agreed after I wrote a poem or three to get
these published and share my thoughts with you, the
public.

I owe everything I have to God and thank Him in
a little way by mentioning Him in my verses. The
people I have written for, to, or about have always
said "Thanks-a-lot". They know the words I use come
from my heart.

CONTENTS

Preface..xv

A Friend, What Else Would You Call Him?.................................. 1-3

This poem is for a Beautiful Sweet Skinny Lovely Mommy..................... 1-5

Memories... 1-7

Neighbors 1-9

A Very Short Time 2-13

Anniversary Song 2-15

Anniversary Song (Con't) 2-17

Apparently 2-19

Destiny Brought Us Together... 2-21

Happy Birthday Karin... 2-23

Just When 2-25

Love is More 2-27

A Day for Mothers... 2-29

Reverse Blues (use 12 bar blues) 2-31

Small Bouquets 2-33

"Would You?" 2-35

Yellow Rose... 2-37

A Good Plan 3-41

Don't Let Negative Opinions Sway You.. 3-43

Recipe for the Ideal Father.. 3-45

Frustration 3-47

If God Was a She.. 3-49

If There Is A Way to Pass Up This Day... 3-51

Make Sense? 3-53

Nature Calls You Listen... 3-55

Lyrics for Let There Be Peace On Earth.. 3-57

Roses are Dead 3-59

Stranger with Roving Eyes... 3-61

Support... 3-63

You May Wonder 3-65

A Wedding Wish 4-69

The Janus Family Has Something to Celebrate 4-71

Congratulate Stan 4-73

Dad 4-75

Great Work 4-77

My Granddaughter Gidget is being Baptized Today 4-79

To Ron & Vikki Forever 4-81

Ron proposed to you 4-83

Stan 4-85

What a Catch I'm Sure You Both Will Agree 4-87

Welcome Home Jim 4-89

Words of Wisdom Written on a Napkin 4-91

Because Why Daddy? 5-95

Christine Is In The Hospital 5-97

Dad Was the Reason 5-99

Poems are Easy 5-101

It's a GIRL!!! 5-103

"Just a Baby?!!!!" 5-105

One Year Then Another 5-107

One Year Then Another (Con't) 5-109

Rick's Submarine 5-111

Susan 5-113

I Don't Need Much To Make My Thanksgiving 5-115

Princess Pillow 5-117

To Pat 5-119

Word to the Wise 6-123

Years Fly By 6-125

A True Lady's 90th Birthday 7-129

Happy Birthday Ron 7-131

Meaghan is 4 This Year 7-133

Happy Birthday to Clara for Whom We All Doth Cara 7-135

Jessica is 4 This Year 7-137

Karin on Your Birthday 7-139

Margret's 6th 7-141

Vikki, It's Your Birthday Today 7-143

This calls for a special cheer 7-145

Tom's Birthday 7-147

Get Well Bob 8-151

Get Well Fast Donna.. 8-153
Tribute to you Vikki... 8-155
Don't Worry... 9-159
To Honor Joe 9-161
A Concrete Story... 10-165
Accolade for Nate.. 10-167
Accolades to Dr. Dave' 10-169
David.. 10-171
Dr. Kock "A Blessing to His Chiropractic Profession"........................ 10-173
For All You Do... 10-175
Good Mechanics are hard to find 10-177
If He Fixed My Problem Omar Can Fix Anybody's 10-179
Thanks Greg Milburn 10-181
Thanks Nancy.. 10-183
Dave the Tax Man.. 10-185
Up Above Will Trim Your Tree 10-187
Ode to Carlton Hall 10-189

Preface

If You Are Reading This You Bought My Book . . . Thanks
*As I look at my career I find it quite **diverse***
*I will try to put part of this in **verse***

I started at Emerson Electric as an illustrator
After graduating from a community college
*In the **Technical Illustrator** program*

I helped to develop plans for the mounting of the
Mini-tat machine gun on helicopters. Right-a-way I
Had a mentor he was their best artist

Emerson was not hiring full-time employees so I worked at
McDonnell Aircraft from 12/6/1971 until 9/30/1990

I had a distinguished run until a 5,000 worker layoff made me look
*Elsewhere for gainfull employment. **While I was home***
I made a living on the phone

I sold ads the size of business cards on maps to vendors to keep their
Names on the minds of their customers

I found a way to increase their thirst
By giving them an opportunity to improve their
Chances of being called first

Later I learned the business of dressing up in costumes
For children's birthday parties: ninja turtles, Easter Bunny
In malls and a large brown bear to promote sales campaigns

As a ninja turtle I made balloon animals, hats, swords,
Special requests, I even came up with a way to make
A bicycle for my granddaughters. That was the best

I learned the business of decorating with balloons. As an artist I
Could use my skills to make miniature displays to show customers
I could make their wedding, party and anything they wanted to
Decorate for better with balloons. I made a presentation to the Navy

For a roof-top celebration it was looked upon with great anticipation.

I worked for the local cable company in installation, sales and repair.
I went back to college to learn AutoCad. Now I could get a job in
Industry again and make more money while I was there.

I did illustrations for sewing machine catalogues and a boiler maker
Who produced a system that could make electricity anywhere in the world.

Money was good again until . . .

I forgot how to use a computer entirely surprising everyone, including
Me. I believe all my disabilities started then and have been getting
Worse ever since. Now I find myself happier getting this book to
Print. It is a God given talent, I prayed to Him for help I could use.

I have to give Him credit because without God there would not be this
Book to mention. This story is hard to believe I know but the events in
My life are true. **"You can't make this stuff up"**, I must thank God
And my wonderful supporting wife for thier intervention.
I sincerely hope this gets your attention.

I hope I can do book 2, and if the readers agree number 3.

A Friend, What Else Would You Call Him?

I've got a buddy who is the true measure of what a friend
Should be. If you ask him for a favor, he won't say well
I'll . . . I'll check and see maybe I can do it

The true measure of a friend is a man like Ben. He says **where?**
And when? There are not many people in this world like him.
I am just fortunate to know him

I'd recommend him to everyone that I know, but I am sure he
Wouldn't have time. I can keep him pretty busy, you know?
He is a good person, he never asks for anything in return

He just does what he does and to me he is the real measure of
A friend. Don't get the wrong idea; I pay him back by doing
Things for him that he would not do for himself

I have made him a model of his favorite truck. He used to take
To car shows and parades. I made it exact in every way right
Down to the license plate

He displays it in his garage for everyone to see he says **"No**
One ever cared enough to do something like that for me." I
Have repaid his generosity in more ways too. So I will stop
Before I bore you

This poem is for a **Beautiful Sweet Skinny Lovely Mommy**
Like you who are to good to be true

Although I am physically uncomfortable to drive there to you
My thoughts will always be with you

I am surprised to know that you are in a nursing home but
I am sure you are getting the best of care
Because someone like you deserves it there

When I called and got Markus on the phone
I was trying to find out if Joe would be home

On that day I got the surprise of my life when I heard him say
You were in the hospital and did not know how long you would stay

I only write poems to the ones I love and you are at the top of the list
Only Karin, my kids, and grand kids are above

Get better soon my prayers are with you I get them answered when I
Pray for other people
Maybe that's why I am drawn to a church
With a great big steeple

I don't know what the future holds for us
I pray that you will be back home with us

It is not fair that you have caller ID
I can't surprise you anymore and
Call you **Beautiful Sweet Skinny Lovely Mommy**
Since you will already know it's me

Memories

47 years is a long time to have a friend. After I introduced Rick to Hank, Butch and Ken he brought my arch enemy to my house but how was I to know then you would become my best friend?

Before you there was Mike whom you despised at the time, but grew to be his friend too over time. You and he smoked, drank and we went to the Ozark show together looking for girls.

You, Mike and Bill went in the Navy together. Little did you know that the buddy system only meant you would be in the same Navy together. I went to college, but we still stayed in touch. I visited you in Maryland to see you while you were in the Ceremonial Honor Guard. That was the best place they could have put you, because you were always so picky about how you looked. You couldn't pass up a mirror.

My parents loved you, even my dad. I can still hear those immortal words. **"Good night Tony** it's 2:00 in the morning **go home"** You weren't sure if he liked you or not.

Remember when we used to spend our time late in the morning playing 500 Rummy, drawing crazy pictures that dad did not understand, because you drew yours with monstrous creatures coming thru the roof with a broken Hurst stick shift in his hand. We would listen to KXOK oldies with Johnny Rabbit.

Years came and went you had your romances and I had mine, on these I will not lament. Now our lives are great I found Karin and you found Dee. On this you will have to agree.

They are the best for us. They are what keeps us going and together with them, We have raised a great family, and our happiness we owe to them.

I love you Tony that's something I seldom say to a guy, but it sums up the feelings between you and I. Friends Always, Bob

P.S. You are more like the other brother I never had.

Neighbors

It sure would be nice to have
Neighbors to talk to

It sure would be nice to have
Neighbors to confide in

It sure would be nice to have
Neighbors to watch your house

It sure would be nice to have
Neighbors to share interests with

It sure would be nice to have
Neighbors to do little things for

It sure would be nice to have
Neighbors to play cards with

It sure would be nice to have
Neighbors to share costs of having work done

It sure would be nice to have
Neighbors to ask for a favor and not have them reject me

Hey wait a minute
I have all that and it is just my luck

They live next door

A Very Short Time

To some 36 years seems like a long time.
It would be if like some it seems like a sentence

To me it is not like that at all.
It seems to be quite small not a sentence at all

Life with you has been so easy, because you make
Big problems seem small

No matter how I have pleaded with you
You don't let me take some of the burden large or small

You were always there when I have needed you
You take on responsibility and usually never delegate

My life of love **began** when I met you.
My life of love **flourished** when I married you

My life of love **grows** stronger when I am near you.
My life of loving you for 36 years is still a **short time**

Who Really Loves You Baby?

Anniversary Song

Use the music to John Denver's
Sunshine on my shoulders

Your arms around me make me happy.
Waking up without you makes me cry.
Love light on your face looks so lovely.
Your blonde hair always makes me high

If I had more time that I could give you.
I'd give to you the time that you deserve.
If I had a song that I could write for you,
I'd write a song to show that I love you

Your arms when you hold me make me sigh

Your love almost always . . .

Anniversary Song (Con't)

Use the music to John Denver's
Sunshine on my shoulders

Hugging you in the evening makes me happy.
Being my wife is more than I deserve
Any man out there would trade places.
Knowing you love me makes me sigh . . .

If I had more love that I could give you
I'd give you all the love that I could give
If I had a wish that I could wish for you
It would be to be with you
Thirty-Six more years

I would never grow tired of loving
You this way . . .

Apparently

Apparently *I don't have the words that are
good enough to express the deep Love
I have for you*

Apparently *I don't have the physical strength
to put you high enough on a pedestal
as you deserve*

Apparently *I can't write the song for all to
sing that would raise the rafters high enough to
show my thanks to God for giving you to me*

Apparently *you will just have to settle for a
simple* **"I LOVE YOU"** *from me to you
and thanks for all that you do*

Destiny Brought Us Together

I will always be by your side you can never hide. It all started when you became my bride and I will love you until I die.

You can't escape it. There was never any doubt. Don't even try to figure me out. Or try to change me.

"You knew the job was dangerous when you took it"

I will always love you but love is not a strong enough word to describe the way I feel about you.

I knew the feeling was mutual; you never want to see it end. Neither did I

It would be like losing your best friend, confidant, companion, right arm, the half of your brain that tells you to come in out of the rain and lover

The one you can argue with and never hold a grudge with. I am the guy who will defend you. You are the one that I would die for. On whom you can depend, and never tell a lie for. To gain a means to an end

At first when I saw you I knew that I wanted you the others were just friends after we started dating I knew I would start hating if I passed up a chance to be with you

Best of all I answered the call that brought me to you. Finding out it was mutual made me the happiest I have ever been

I knew if I were to keep you I had to make it known you would be mine and mine alone

I had to monopolize your time and never give the other guys a chance to beat my time; They knew they could not step in and risk taking one on the chin

I had a reputation that I would win, and win I did when I asked you to be mine for all time

Happy Thanksgiving the day I give thanks for you

Your,

Bob Forever

Happy Birthday
Karin

L *Is for the lasting feelings I have for you*

O *is for the ring that I have given to you*
a circle with out end

V *is for value that I feel when I hold you*
in my arms

E *is for eternally being grateful that you*
are who you are

Just When . . .

Just when you think you have said it all
You find out that's just not true

Just when you think you have said it all
You have to come up with something for no. 32

Just when you think you have said it all
You find out that's just not true

You are always in my head and that is where I want you to stay
I love the way you love me in your loving way

Just when you think you have said it all
You find out that's just not true

This one might turn out to be short I don't know what's in my heart
Until I think about and dream about you

Just when you think you have said it all
You find out that's just not true

I have always tried my best to keep you from
Working as hard as you do

Just when you think you have said it all
You find out that's just not true

I know I will never be able to thank you enough, not this **year**, *this* **month** *or this* **week**

Just when you think you have said it all
You find out that's just not true

I will love you always like when I said "I do"

Love is More . . .

Do You Know What Love Is?

Do You Know What Love Is?

Love is not just a Holiday a
Birthday, Anniversary,
Valentine's Day or even Ground hogs day

Love is all the days that come
After or in between

Those other days are nice
They come and go you might think about them twice
They don't make a year as you
Well know

Love is all these things and more
Love is going to the store

Love is helping around the house,
Working together
Love is taking care of one another
To grow older

Love is growing older together
Love is having those memories to share

Love must start before that
Trip down the isle love is forever
Love is what I feel for YOU

A Day for Mothers

If I were to search high and low for a mother
For my children like you there could be no other

A mother who is kind, generous, helpful, truthful and
Always there for them
A mother whom I know will always love them. You're my wife my
Lover and mean the world to me

In these times when people think marriage is trying
Someone out for five years
I can really be confident that you would be here fifty-five
More years on top of our first thirty-six

I look forward to the years watching you with Shannon and all the
Other grand children that our children will rear

I can't explain it but some how the kids have all retained it. You
Made them what they are and made them desirable by far

I know when they made up their minds they were searching
For a spouse like mine

You've instilled in them good habits to be extravagant and generous
To those whom they love part of the time and frugal the
Rest of the time

I hope this mother's day you will reflect on all you have
Accomplished. I know I will, I always have and I still do
Because of those two words **"I DO"** and still would

Reverse Blues (use 12 bar blues)

I met up with Karin this lady of mine.
She threw me on the floor hundreds of times

I taught her self-defense, I let her throw me
Next thing I knew, she was also dating me
Chorus: Now she gave me the reverse blues

I can't get her out of my mind.
I can't get her out of my mind.

We went and got married, everything was fine
We had three children I could call mine
Chorus: Now she gave me the reverse blues

My daughter and her spouse had my granddaughters.
I'm feel' in good I'm feel' in fine

I got the reverse blues, aint got no troubles
With the reverse blues
Chorus: Now she gave me the reverse blues

Small Bouquets

In the past I've dated many girls before I met you
Until we met, I never dated a woman like you

You are the woman who means everything to me
You are the woman who does everything with me and for me

You have always been there and stood by me
I hate to think what my life would be if I'd never met you

These flowers to men don't mean much, but to a woman they mean
So . . . o much and you're not a woman who expects much

A small bouquet of spring flowers instead of a large bouquet
Of the most expensive roses

You always do what you can for our family it goes beyond love
More like dedication to keep everybody happy

That night when you invited me to your house to cook me a simple
Spaghetti dinner

I knew I wouldn't starve.
I knew you were a winner

There is so much I could tell you but that would only embarrass you,
Because you are not one to take too much praise

So maybe I will keep giving you small bouquets

"Would You?"

Would you still stick by me no
Matter what the circumstances?

Would you still be frugal
With our finances?

Would you be as loving
To my parents
As you are to your own?

Would you still be a loving
Wife and mother to our
Children at home?

Would you always be there
To dry my tears?

Would you always be unselfish
And supportive for 30 years?

Would you still love me
Through good times and in bad?

Would you remember the
Beautiful wedding we had?

Would you still have so
Much difficulty
Saying goodnight at the door?

Would you believe me when
I say?
"You are the one that I adore"

Would you be satisfied to
Have each other's company
On a date?

Would you still marry me
And make me feel great?

Would you still say, "I do"
At our wedding?

Would you agree to another
30 years of not regretting?

Love & Adoration Bob
April 12, 2005

Yellow Rose

If I were to write a poem about roses
It would start out roses are red

Since I want to say I love you
And only you
I'll use just one yellow rose instead

If a rose is to remain a bud and
Never open
It's just like young love,
Desired by one, and never spoken

However if rose is allowed to bloom and
flourish it can do no more than nourish

The wonderful feelings of love
I have for You

A Good Plan

Today is a computer day.
My hands are sore and I can't work that other way

What I mean to say is the scooter will have to wait.
While I charge the batteries

Any testing I do will come out with good results using;
Methods that are tried and true

I will spend the day writing poems,
Formatting pages and talking to my publisher
About my style

That will keep me busy for quite awhile
I have questions for them before I proceed,

And do something unnecessary I won't even need
To yield the best product you will ever read

Don't Let Negative Opinions
Sway You

I saw this hat in Branson
The people who were there said I looked handsome

They were not sales people as you might cajole, they
Were honest people on the street
I will have you know

My wife liked it too that is all I
Needed to make my decision go through

So I bought it and I still wear it, if you don't like it
It doesn't matter to me because I do

If I wear it with guitar in hand
All I can say is it makes me feel grand

Recipe for the Ideal Father

* Take one man who loves your mother
* Would rather be with **you** than at work
* Does not hang out in a bar drinking
   with the guys
* Takes you on vacations where **you**
   want to have fun
* Will accept **you** for yourself and not force **you**
   to be his image of what you should be

**Let the mixture stand while you add the
important ingredients:**

Love, dedication, unselfishness, helping hand,
Teacher, advisor, disciplinarian, role model,
Protector, honesty and treats you like himself

Pour mixture into the Ideal Father mold and keep
Him close to your heart for life

Frustration

I bought some diamond earrings today.
To say the experience was joyful is a lie I could not say

I was on the phone not for an hour, two, or even three but
Four comes to mind.
It turned a guy who is usually easy to please into one that
Was frustrated and not feeling too kind

I found I was being batted around from department to
Department and email to email.

This turned me into a person whom
Was not good to be around

It was finally settled when I asked to speak
To a supervisor, I thought.

I waited two weeks before I called back to find out my order
Still was not bought

They did not give me enough credit that day. I ask you

How did they think I could buy what I wanted with
Only the amount they authorized?

If God Was a She

What if God is a she?

She could make this a woman's world and all men would
    See finally there is no glory in a war
    Fought where both sides lose their most precious resource,
    The children of this world

What if God is a she?
    She would be a fair God, an always there God
    Remind us of our free will God
    To make us realize there really are two sides to every issue

We need to think more about what a woman would do in a situation
    And not be **competitive, stingy, liars and cheats** like we have in political
Offices who say that God must be a man and let the devil
    Gain the upper hand;

What if God is a she?
    She would really be able to put one over on me

What if God is a she?
    She could know what men and men like me would need

What if God is a she?
    Illness like mine could be a joke and when I wake one day I could find hope

What if God is a she?
    I might be punished for my past like the other men like me who didn't believe
    The punishment would last

What if God is a she?
    The women I've known would kick me off my self appointed throne

What if God is a she?
    She would make me see the female side of many issues I would then know
    Why they go through so many tissues

If There Is A Way to Pass Up This Day

I am a smart driver
I wish there were more
Like me

The drivers are crazy
Or am I just lazy

I want to drive at
My leisure
But the clock and drivers
Won't let me alone

I'd rather be home I am not
Accustomed to this
Frenzy anymore

They may raise a finger,
That doesn't bother me

Because now I am safely in
The lane where I wanted

To be. There is plenty of
Room **they can go around me**

They won't let me over or
Get out of my blind spot,
Which seems to be all over

Here comes a Landrover
I had better move over
No! I will let him use his
Brakes instead

I will use my out of state, I
Don't know what I am
Doing act. That will slow
Them all down

Therefore, I can drive where
I want to in this town

Vindictive you say, Is there
Another way? **Na I don't
Think so, not today**

Make Sense?

A strange occurrence happened today
It struck me in a most unusual way

I was at the dentist and they put cards in my mouth and
Said "bite down" and just went away

I said as best I could "where are you going?"
They replied, "to protect myself from the x ray"

So here I am with cards and a lead blanket on me and they run away to
Another room. I think with no regards for my safety from the x rays.

It went through my head they were surrounded completely with lead
With no regard for my head

I'm sure you have been through this, but they assure you, you don't
Need your head protected

Unless you are using a cell phone the people who sell phones don't
Bother to tell you about radiation

Instead they just say you can use this on your vacation

Nature Calls You Listen

Nature is calling
To some it is quite appalling

Sometimes it is lenient
Most times, it is inconvenient

You gotta answer
Or fill your pants there
When you are on your way anywhere

It will give you disappointment
Because you want to be there for your appointment

It is nice to have a phone
When you leave home

Because this way
You can let them know you are on the way

I'm usually not fond of a cellular
However, it will get there ahead of you
In addition, take all the stress off you

If that is, all you use it
You won't abuse it

Everyone is happy you thought of them when you get there

Lyrics for Let There Be
Peace On Earth
(Sy Miller & Gill Jackson)

THE *PROMISE*

Let me write my poetry
and share it with my fellow man

Let these words touch everyone
and this is my fondest plan

To teach each man to be good to a
woman and each woman to
love her man

Let me bring joy to earth and
happiness to all my friends

**Let this teach adolescents right for
this is a parent's plight**

**Help them be serious in love and be
favored by God above**

**To make men more sensitive to
how a woman feels**

**I share poems to all people my
experience will show them how**

Let me share my poems to those
who care about past, future and
right now

Give me the insight Lord in spite
of my illness please

Help me use true life examples to
guide them to do right

I'll write these poems and show
them how your life has touched me
now. Help me reach them somehow

**Help me write my poetry and
strengthen me for the future
to come**

**I have married a terrific woman
and we raised our children
geniuses are all three**

**I owe my thanks and gratitude to
no one else but thee
They are all good people and have
spouses that will agree**

Let me write my poetry and share
this gift with thee
(final raise key)
This is the promise I make to
forever honor you my Lord

Help me write these poems to bring
people closer to you my God

Roses are Dead

Roses are dead and violets aren't for you
Give me a moment to study you

I will come up with a poem that is right for you

It might be funny it might be sad
It will be made up with the thoughts I have had

Give me 15 minutes and I will choose
Words that I can write for you

When I write a poem, my pain subsides because God
Gave me this ability. I am distracted
From the torment

So if this sells well
I will do it again to save me from this living Hell

Stranger with Roving Eyes

Roving eyes and unknown wishes at this time get me in trouble if she
Truly knew my mind

If only she wasn't accompanied by such a large husband

I could make my thoughts be known

He is watching my eyes, I feel it but that won't keep me from looking
Right straight at her and I mean it, that won't stop me, no sir ree

I can stand a little pain because it's worth it

Experience tells me if you look at ten

One would be worth it again and again

Good looking women are hard to find

That is why they are always on my mind

I hope this one is sweet and kind

My eyes get me in trouble all the time. If she knew my wishes
I should have stayed home and did the dishes

Support

I met two people today and
It was wonderful I have to say
Talking to a husband and wife
Who were old and gray

They proved to me what I knew already
She was the strong one
And he was not steady

It hurt him to rise to his feet
Trying to see what I was sketching
With just a ballpoint and a
Picture of a woman in a magazine

I could see pain in his face
But it was not a disgrace
I apologized to him and I stood up instead
Even though sometimes
It hurts to get out of my own bed

Behind every man who is happily married
Is a woman supportive and caring

You May Wonder

Why something this important was left up to men to decide

You may wonder why

You don't hear a baby cry

You may wonder why

You don't hear a baby sigh

You may wonder why

There are no baby tears to dry

You may wonder why

You don't hear the pitter patter of a baby's feet

Wearing baby shoes

You may wonder why

I will tell you the heart wrenching truth

This baby never had a chance to LIVE

Nobody will stop a word that to most has lost
*The true meaning it's **Abortion** and it means **Dead***
*And ladies it is **final***

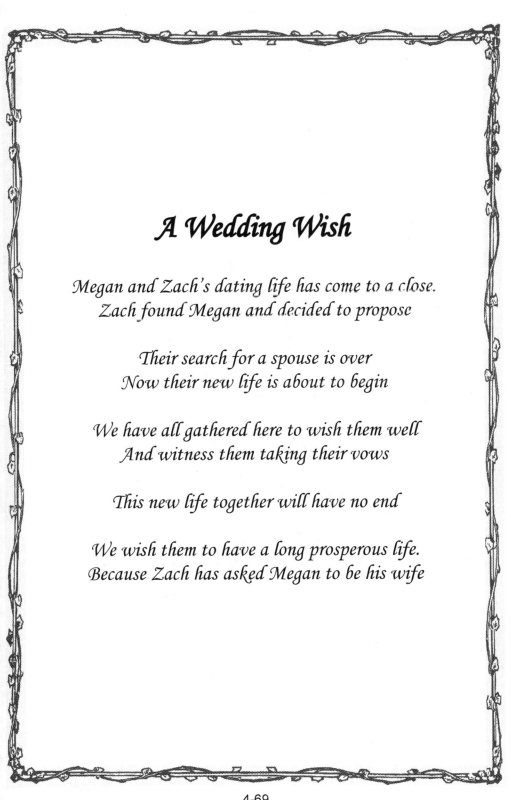

A Wedding Wish

Megan and Zach's dating life has come to a close.
Zach found Megan and decided to propose

Their search for a spouse is over
Now their new life is about to begin

We have all gathered here to wish them well
And witness them taking their vows

This new life together will have no end

We wish them to have a long prosperous life.
Because Zach has asked Megan to be his wife

The Janus Family Has Something to Celebrate

Or may I reiterate the Beyer's
Beverly has decided to retire

From the U.S. Coast Guard it will be
So we all decided to come and
Celebrate with thee

She served her country well and of this,
She can always tell
She gave 35+ years to the land of the free
As a Senior Chief

Her husband Jay did the same and
Retired as a Captain

At one time I was told she out ranked him
"A man will work from sun to sun"
Beverly's work will never be done

Even though she has retired,
I forgot to mention
She would now receive a nice pension

Let's congratulate them both by giving them a
Toast to thank them for all they have done

In sincerest devotion from
Her family, Jay's family, my family and I

Congratulate Stan

To Stan we should congratulate
Because he has graduated

He has always been a good student
In grade school he was always prudent

Since the other High Schools didn't show him
Math books that would challenge him

He set goals for himself and those goals where met
He told me that was why he chose DeSmet

He always took the honors courses they would be hard and he knew it
In his mind, he knew he could do it

Only he can say why he went to Rolla
To learn Computer Science

Then he made a wiser choice to stick it out
Another half year to be a Computer Engineer

Through Grade school, High and College
He has gained that precious knowledge

I told him in the long run it would pay off for him
Now large companies are after him

I know he is destined to go farther
I am proud of him, but I still can't rest, guiding him to do his best
For after all I am his father

Dad

Welcome to the club we call Dad
It is not so illusive
In fact, it's quite exclusive
You can be the best one we ever had

All it takes to be there
Is to recognize the need there
And always be willing to give your time

You'll get the feeling that is so appealing
When you do what you auter
For your brand new daughter

A daughter, you will find
Can drive you out of your mind
But don't you fret it you will never regret it
If you have a daughter like mine

She will have all kinds of reasons
To keep her clothes in season
They think money grows on trees
In addition, it comes to you with ease

Soon they will find sometimes it's hard to be kind
You will always protect her you can never reject her

You will pay for a wedding
Never forgetting
Moreover, hope you will be getting a son-in-law like mine

It makes life worth living when a flower you are given

Stay on the path your on. It's a win win situation

Next time it might be carnations

I keep pictures and remembrances of you

I can keep up the rhyme if you put in your time

Losing the weight is not easy keeping it off is hard

You are doing great just using the bike

I felt you deserved a little compensation for your dedication

If you lose ten more it will be off to the store for clothes

Don't be impatient!!

Great Work

My Granddaughter Gidget is being Baptized Today

This Sacrament will make Gidget
Perfect in every way
She is not just a blessing to us, but God will make her
Perfect in His way

This will be her best day
She will be free of Original sin
As far as heaven goes
Nothing can keep her from getting in

She will receive another set of parents to
Help her get there

Someone else she can be close to
Someone else to guide her there

Someone else to love her as Karin and I do
And her other grandparents Ben & Joan do

Life is not easy and no one knows the future, but she
Has a good start with a family who loves her
And godparents like Vikki & Travis to support her

We will always love you Gidget
Paw Paw Bob & Grandma Karin 10/24/2010

To Ron & Vikki Forever

Ron is a man of character and we are as proud
Of him as a mom and dad can be
There is a special place for him in our hearts I'm
Sure you'd agree

He is intelligent, conscientious, thorough
And a joy to be with and forever caring
What more could Vikki ask for in a man
In whose life she will be forever sharing

As our family has come to know Vikki
We have learned she is a very sweet, unselfish
And loving person who doesn't make bad choices

She will be the perfect selection for our son's
Affection. She will be the perfect wife for Ron
And he will be the best husband for her

So raise your glasses as we toast
To two people who love each other the most
To Ron and Vikki Post

Ron proposed to you

Try to remember that time in December
When both of you were talking about marriage

Little did you know . . . ?

When you were talking about it over and over
Ron already had his mind made up to win you over

He would ask you to be his wife
To spend with you the rest of his life

We knew that you were the one
You would bring joy to him for years to come

It is great that your parents love Ron like they do
Because we love you too

So never, forget the day
That he proposed to you

Stan

Stan is at Rolla and this I can holla
I am proud to be the fatha of him

In my words I can say I am proud this day
He has accomplished two majors and a minor
Computer Science, Engineering and Math

He will contribute and some will pay tribute
To what he has done while he was there

He will contribute on our behalf
To what he knows of computers and math

He has always been a good son
A do what he should son
I always knew he would succeed son

Stan now has Clara and he feels like Yogi Berra
After winning a close game

That feeling will bring him pleasure
And Clara he will always treasure

He is a true son, a red, white and blue son
I have never regretted to go for three

I hold in my heart a special part reserved for just he

What a Catch I'm Sure You Both Will Agree

John is a man of character
Moreover, I am as proud of him as a dad can be

I hold a special place for him in my heart
He is caring, conscientious, thorough, and smart

What more could Vikki ask for in
Whose life she will be forever sharing

As our family has come to know Vikki
We have learned she is a very sweet, unselfish, caring, and
Diligent person (good cook too)

Who goes after what she wants until he catches her she will
Be the perfect choice as his wife and he as her husband

She will be good for John and him for her

So raise your glasses as we toast
To many years of happiness to the two getting married
This coming day October 27th

To the best that God can give to John and Vikki

Welcome Home Jim

Congratulations to you Jim you have made it an honor to watch you
Grow and to enjoy knowing your father and mother as best friends

Jim we watched you grow and make your choice to let the **Army**
Make a man out of you

We were sad when you left that day for Iraq we were all surprised
When you decided to learn about fuel

But in the long run it was wise there will always be a need for
Someone knowledgeable about all kinds of fuel

Whether it is gasoline or aircraft fuel or rocket fuel you found
Yourself a skill to be proud of and make a job of

We celebrate that your time in the army is through
You have an Honorable Discharge that is true
You are surrounded by those who love you

Welcome home now you can help your dad finish that project
All three of you had . . . **LIGHTNING (39 Chevy)**

When you finish it you will be proud because
You did it together and be able to shout out loud

"I did it with my dad and brother"!

So welcome home and good luck take what you have learned about the
Chemicals and put it to good use

So we won't have to rely on this gasoline for our future use
Love and Happiness Always Bob & Karin

Words of Wisdom
Written on a Napkin

Greg this poem I wrote is for
You and Michelle

Anyone who knows you and her
Knows you married well

Love and cherish the best
Friend you've got

Take it from me
I have been married for 33

Always love her and she will comfort you
And she will always care for you

Because Why Daddy?

Because when you need a friend
There will always be Ken

Because when you need a lover
I'm sure that one he can cover

Because when you need your dad
If you are feeling bad

Because there is no other just ask your mother
Who will comfort you like me

Because if you are feeling good like
You always should

Because I will enjoy it
Share it with me

Because you will be a new mother
And I will have a granddaughter
That will be like no other

Because I Love You

That's why

Christine Is In The Hospital You See

Giving birth to our
Granddaughter Ear-ly

The name that struck me
Made them both agree

The best one came from me
So Margret Marie she will be

I could write more
But I must be out the door

To deliver this with a card on a gift
And with a kiss for sure

Dad Was the Reason

Dad was the reason because he is still in my heart
Whenever I take a car apart

I learned from a mechanic's mechanic. He fixed cars, raced cars
Made parts, and did not just replace parts

Between 14-18 I myself worked with him on cars.
I think that qualifies me to be a good judge of a mechanic's character

He would always do his best for a customer at a fair price.
You could always be sure he would stay that way.
Customers kept coming back that way

If he moved to another station
Customers would seek him out at his new location

Dad was so meticulous there will not be
Any fly crap in pepper with him around

That is where I get it. If jobs are worth doing, they must be done right
That is why I have this poem to write

Poems are Easy

Poems are easy some would say
If you write them sincerely they are better that way

I could write them each day
It helps to pass the time away

Christine gave birth to my granddaughter
She followed the plan just like she auter

When it was time she went in a scurry
The baby was born ten days early

Mothers are easy sons keep me busy
To them it is meant as true sentiment

Boys would not cry so easy
They have been known to embarrass easy

Because it is harder
Than just sending a card or two

They are all impressed
When they read the rest

It made them feel good
Like I knew it would

It's a GIRL!!!

Well Marie it was **WONDERFUL** the day you were born I
remember it clearly, because your mother had a hold of my arm

When you were born, I could see clearly a tear rolled down my cheek
when my eyes saw, in my joy, you were not a boy

That tear you see was attached to my heart. I'll always remember
that day. Your mom waited patiently for them to bring you

**Therefore, she could feed you
I waited** impatiently. **Just so I could hold you.**

I think that as you grew up we were more than just father and
daughter, **we were friends.** That's a lot to say these days.
I have loved all the time I could spend with you

I've always been proud of you. I always talk about you when we are
out. I talk about the boys because I am proud of them too

You have given me special things. Three comes to mind
granddaughters is what I find when I come to visit you

Thank you Ben and Marie for being good parents. I hope the
closeness we had when you were young continues as you
mature and teach your young.

I hope that your mother and I have made an impression on you
to raise them to be as good as you I LOVE you, your Dad

"Just a Baby?!!!!"

Margret likes her butt patted
Margret likes her back patted

Margret likes to bounce on your knee
Grandpa loves her and he does it for free

What she likes best is to rest on my chest
It is a good thing too it is exactly what I like to do

Telling her not to cry brings a tear to my eye
Margret reaches deep into me every time she looks at me

She will really make an impression
When you see all of her expressions

First, she will yawn a little
Then she will yawn a lot

Then comes the smile that's meant
She is quite content

She will stare at you with her baby blues
She already knows the power that she's got

She is just a baby you might say
Yes, but extraordinary in every way

One Year Then Another

music to fiddler on the roof (sunrise sunset)

One day Clara asked Stan to take her to
her prom

Stan said he would love to be with her

After that they stayed together always dating
and hanging around

Chorus One year then another, One year then
another quickly they went by

One restaurant and movie after another

Finishing school was on both of their minds

They did it smart Stan chose computers, Clara
decided to be a neonatal nurse

Chorus One year then another, One year then
another quickly they went by

One Year Then Another
(Con't)

They dated for years and stayed
   together Stan chose to buy a house in KC

He was making a nest for them both and
   Clara agreed
   Chorus: One year then another, One year
   then another quickly they went by

Now they have chosen to do the best thing

Under God's eyes they will be known as
   man & wife

Their parents couldn't be happier
   We know they are prepared for this
   new life

   Chorus: One year then another, One year
   then another quickly they go by

Rick's Submarine

A gift to you while you are convalescing
You will say to yourself this is a blessing

Instead of lounging around and sitting on your ass
You can put this to good use and catch some bass

You can get fresh air and sun enjoying the deck you built
And if you get cleaver you can set different depths
On two treble hooks

You could also make a line with lore in the rear
And if you get a lungcer, luncker, lungker, oh heck **BIG FISH** Rick
You can shout for all to hear

Rick everyone will think you are nuts playing
With a toy submarine just tell them you are testing it for the
Navy Seals and a covert application

Then watch them roll their eyes in you general direction
Explain to them that worse thinking than that has ruined our nation
Have fun I love You

Susan

Happy Birthday to this cousin of mine
I think about her all of the time

It's not my willingness that keeps me away
It's this illness that taunts me each day

I have a lot of fond memories
Of the days in Fenton, Ozark and Branson

I have been lucky these past months my daughter
Gave me a beautiful granddaughter instead of a grandson

Her name is Margret Marie
And she is a joy to see

If distance were not my enemy
I could visit you, Mike, Terri, Dorothy and Jeremy

I'm sure you would like to share with me
A great big bowl of chicken and dumplings

Just like the ones
You used to prepare for me

I will never forget frog fries at Bull creek
Or the poker games that would last all week

The 4th of July will never be the same
As it was when all the Purcell's came

So here is a wish that may come true
I wish to come down and be with YOU

I Don't Need Much To Make
My Thanksgiving

Maybe I will have a little turkey
Maybe I will have a little dressing

Mashed potatoes and gravy to top it off
Maybe I will have a little sweet potatoes
With marshmallows

Maybe I will have a little cranberry sauce
Maybe I will have a little waldorf salad

Green bean casserole and a buttered dinner roll would
Be nice yeh! That would suffice

Something is missing, what could it be? It is my
Wonderful **wife** entire **family,** best **friends** and **grand**
Children. The **noise** from the clamour of everyone
Rooting for a **football game, caroling,** and **dancing** it's
All the same

But without thanking God for all that, I have the
Rest, it would not mean the same to me without
Giving thanks to Him
And praying that He be kind
To the less fortunate at this time

See I don't need much to make my thanksgiving, Do you?

Princess Pillow

A pillow for your head
When you just want the bed,
Put up your feet instead

As a new mom you will be there.
You have another mouth to feed there

When you need a friend,
On dad, you can depend

When you need an ear,
I will always be here

You won't always see me,
However, I think you'll agree with me

I'd rather be with you instead.
Like the pillow that's under your head . . .

Love Dad

To Pat

I wish you comfort with
Your children and peace of mind
In your new life

This is not an end it's a new beginning
Accept the gifts that God has given to you

I wish enough money to
Forget your worries

I wish you a **Great Big** *hug from your mother,*
Sisters and brother

And another hug from your brother-in-law
I wish you the best of
Everything large and small

How to Treat a Lady

Word to the Wise

If you marry for beauty and beauty alone
I'm afraid that one I can't condone. You have to marry
Her because she is your friend, she's smart,
She is closer to you than your own heart

Being without her is like living alone
Knowing she will be there is what makes a happy home.
Sure she is gorgeous coming down that aisle
Beauty is fleeting love is not that is why you have
Come to her to tie the knot

She is not a plaything she is the other half of you
When you have children, they will look at the way you
Treat your wife that is how they will look at life

Nevertheless, you have to look at it this way **"love has no Beginning love has no end"** (from vows)
That's why you give her a ring as a symbol that your love
Will never end

You never know what the future will bring
You will grow older together and promise your bride you
Will always be at her side

This is a word to the wise

Years Fly By

Who would have known that, that first kiss would
Lead to years of happiness and bliss

I'm sure you will agree because it comes from me

Be happy that you have each other
No one else would love you like you love each other

Ben you always said I could pick out cards that met
The occasion
I think a 10-year anniversary is a reason
For celebration

If I had a glass, I would lift it to toast you
I would say congratulations and have everyone
Present wish for continued love and the most of
Everything that is good for you

Ben is a protective father and Marie a wonderful
Mother. Happy Anniversary! I'm looking for another
10 for Marie and Ben

A True Lady's 90ᵗʰ Birthday

Cora it is not something that I
Would always do but, in your case because you are you

I feel comfortable calling you **mom** after I lost mine
That is what you have been to me all this time

I was a staunch catholic. A server too, until high school and
College ruined that too

I met your daughter and the rest of your family.
By your example, you got me back to church **for the first time**

Then in my life and through the strife
I took your daughter for my wife.
She was as kind and generous as you were.
You taught her well that reflects on you

She and you got me through. You didn't know it
Your example showed it.
You made me want to please her and you.
And got me back for **time number two**

If anybody gets her wings, it should be you. You saved me twice.
I have never met anyone as nice

Thank you with all my love

Happy Birthday Ron

Poems for you I have written before
I thought it might be difficult to
Find more

You proved that life goes on
You marry your wife
Before you know it she gives birth to
A new life

Rose comes to mind every time
Ron and Vikki comes to mine

Thoughts about how good it feels to be a
Grandpa again in my lifetime

Meaghan is 4 This Year

Meaghan this one is **4** you
We celebrate your birthday too

Every year at this time, we set aside special time
To have a party **4** you

You are a little lady always
Dressing up and looking pretty

Your way to have fun
Is to dress up and show everyone

You are as pretty inside
As you are outside

Your smile is by **4**
One of your greatest assets so **4**

It has the power to melt the hearts
Of everyone around you

So **4** today we celebrate your birthday **4** you

Happy Birthday to Clara for Whom We All Doth Cara

We want her to be happy with Stan and I am sure that
Can be achieved and in her way we doth believe

The smartest move those two made
Was to both have careers that could get a house paid

So they will be able to live life without
Pinching pennies

It may seem corny but all sincerity is meant
Our love for her is shown by us all being here

Now Clara's birthday will be precious to us
When she becomes one of us

The Farley's have a long record of caring
For one another

We are always there for each other no matter
What the circumstances

I'm sure that Stan has made a wise decision to have Clara by his side
After all he has asked her to be his bride

With love Stan's dad and his bride, Karin

Jessica is 4 This Year

Jessica this **1** is **4** you
We celebrate your birthday **2**

Every year at this time
We set aside special time
2 have a party **4** you

You are a little lady always
Dressing up pretty

Your way **2** have fun
Is **2** dress up and show everyone

You are as pretty inside
As you are outside

Your smile is by far
One of your greatest assets so **4**

It has the power **2** melt the hearts
Of everyone around you

So today we celebrate your birthday **4** you

Karin on Your Birthday

I hope this card will brighten your day
Sometimes I don't know what to say

Give me a while to learn a new song
I will play it for you the whole day long

I know that night the stars
Must have been right
They made you for me to share each night

Therefore, may this ditty
Make you feel giddy
Like you were on our honeymoon night

Your Loving Husband
May this witticism stand up to all criticism

Margret's 6th

It's somebody's birthday today
I can't ever forget her
Because I am the one who named her
It's somebody's birthday today

It's somebody's birthday today
Who it is you can't get me to say
We always remember her on this day
It's somebody's birthday today

She's a year older today
We celebrate every year on this day
To say happy birthday to you today
Yep it's somebody's birthday today

I can't ever forget her
Because I am the one who named her
It's Margret's birthday today

Vikki, It's Your Birthday Today

I feel like I can say it best

Because I know your first request,
I couldn't give you a better present

Than the one . . .
After all, you have chosen my son

When you have birthdays they come with wishes
It is obvious to me I am not a miracle worker

However, I can pray to God every day
That all that you ask for will come your way

Another year will pass and day after day, I pray
You and Don will be fortunate in every way

You're my new daughter and I'm your new dad
Happy birthday Mrs. Purcell I wish you well
Love Dad

This calls for a special cheer   *(from Saturday Night Live)*
To help you celebrate this year

Today it's your birthday
You will probably stop count' in them today

Gotta remember the years passed by
Cause the rest of them will just fly

You have had a wonderful life so far
A lovely wife, two great kids and that fancy car

Every time you look at our photograph
You'll remember Karin and me
Wrapped a gift for you

And gave fifty dollars to Sharon
To spend on you

I wish that I could drink and share a case
Of beer or two

If I did that, we would only have one evening to
Celebrate this year with you

This gift we give to you it will let you enjoy your Movies,
Radio, computer, and your TV too

So we tell you happy birthday Ben and
Wish you 54 more

*If we searched, the world over we'd never find a friend **like you . . . ore***

Tom's Birthday

Hey Tom all I have to say is happy birthday but no you
Deserve more than that

You have been a great husband and father
And a mechanic at that

Judy can depend on you and your sons are included in that too
You have always had a kind greeting for me and my family

I could sum it up in a word. But a word would never do.
A book maybe

I can't think of enough stories to put in it
However if you were the teller

I could probably put it into rhyme but I am going to wait
Until later I can't do it this time

Tim and Dave will always be proud of their father
And Judy will always love her husband

And somehow you just can't stop working for car dealers;
They just keep asking you back

Well happy birthday I am honored to share this one with you
And many more "I'll be back "if you ask me to

Get Well Bob

I only write poems to those
Whom I care about

In a way they are the
Way I pray
Evidently God is a fan of poetry
Because He listens and
Will help the friends like thee

When I talk to God on your behalf
It gives me hope that you will be back

It's my way of saying I will keep on praying
Until you come home

I miss coming out of the house and trading
A greeting

Whether it is to say "Hi" or "Good Bye"
It's just what friendly neighbors do

It will be great to wave it to you, *Bob & Karen*

Get Well **Fast** Donna

To the best friend a neighbor can have
From the best friend a neighbor can have

I will be looking forward to your return
In your case, I will have time to burn

We will be keeping your computer and printer running
I think I can help when your printer is out of ink

We will continue to trade books
About aircraft I think

I have pictures of the prologue room, just ask
They contain the wonderful work of John's craft

When I say, **"let me know if you need help"** I mean it
I have been there when you needed me to
keep your printer printing and computer putering

And your e-mail available to be
Seen when you want it to be

Your neighbor and friend always, Bob & Karen

Tribute to you Vikki

It's time to get well
So that you I can tell

It's everyone's wishes
To have you back Vikki

My Son is going crazy
Without his wife by his side

That is why he asked you
To be his bride

This family also wishes you were better
That's why I am writing you this letter

As soon as he knew you were in so much pain
He took action to get you well agane

We asked John if we could help
We wanted to let him know you
Are on our minds

He stood there by you as if he was guarding
The most precious person in his life,
And he was !!!!

You will find now that you are part of our family
And if one wheel isn't working, the rest of us are miserable
Until you get well now

Don't Worry

I don't know what to say
except those 3 words
constantly on my mind
"I Love You"

You never get to prepare
You never get to plan

People play the hand that they are dealt
Try to survive the best that they can

When you are playing with that big black jack dealer
In the sky the house always wins even in a tie

I am deeply sorry you couldn't be prepared
But neither was I

I will pray for you from my lofty place in the sky
I have clout with the Big Guy now

To Honor Joe

To Patrick & Shana
I know you will agree with me on what I have to say now

Your father has been a friend to me
A friend that never expected anything back from me

If he could help me with anything
He would always ask to do something

He would always come to my aid
And never expect to be paid

No matter how I pleaded, then he would answer back
With something else he thought I needed

When we were all in our thirty's
And getting together at Christmas parties

He would enjoy going to nursing homes
And sing to the residents about Christmas

He would drive the van and
Never ask for a helping hand

He wouldn't take money
In this day and age that would really be funny

He knew my legs were weak so he gave me a lift chair
That not only lifts my body but lifts my spirits as well

He gave me a trapeze to hang over my bed
So I could reach up and pull myself up instead

I know I will miss him
You kids will never forget him

He and your mother
Were always there for each other

And when you get older you will remember
How he let me cry on his shoulder

A Concrete Story

Give me a moment and I will lament
About a man who works with cement

This poem has only one purpose
It is about a man who will do all he can
To give you what you want and

Also what you need
Money is not the only driving force for him your
Satisfaction for a job well done is the best for him

When all is finished and true you will be thanking
Doug and his crew
When all is said and done you will be proud
To tell and show your friends what
***Doug** has done*
*If you have a job to do call **Doug** at 3145552323*
Any time he will be happy to discuss your job with you
Now a friend Bob Purcell

Doug did not ask for this tribute

Accolade for Nate

To find two mechanics in the same garage
Is unheard of these days.
It would not be right and a terrible over sight

If I did not mention and bring to your attention
Nate at Mullanphy Tire & Automotive
When giving praise
That is so richly deserved and needed these days

Nate has been trained by one of the best.
In my mind he can hold a candle
With the rest of the best

He can get customers and keep customers.
What more could you ask for?

Written by a friend to a friend
Thanks for all the good preventative maintenance on
behalf of my family's safety   Bob Purcell

Accolades to Dr. Dave'

What can you say about the man who is doing everything he can think of to give you a better quality of life? I know I have been trying to find a doctor with the magic pill for over 15 years, I tried; rheumatologists, oncologists, massage therapists, psychologists, psychiatrists, emergency rooms with a pain level of from 1-10 at 15

Some doctors who threw up their hands and wanted me to apply to the Mayo clinic. That is not the way to talk to someone when that someone is looking for hope, at the end of a long relentless tunnel filled with disappointments

It is not that way with Doctor Dave'. He will ask you if the medicine is helping. What helps that is not medicine? Are there any side effects you need help with? Is the pain level bearable? Since you are on narcotics, do you feel like you are addicted? What are your hobbies and when you are engrossed in them, does it seem to help? Do you get support from your family?

Questions like these show me he has a complete interest in my case and wants my quality of life to get better with every report. He will honestly listen. He also wants this book to become a best seller. What a coincidence so do I.

David

David is the man to see when you stop in at
Bob Evans he will treat you like family

A friendlier person you will never meet
A customer he never fails to greet

He will get your order right
If there is an oversight he will make it right

I only write this to prove to him
I have been here before

I have never been dissatisfied
With the service he will provide

When I compared him to the best,
David was hands above the rest

What he doesn't know is this is
The only tip he is going to get

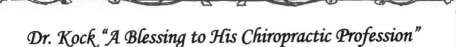

Dr. Kock "A Blessing to His Chiropractic Profession"

There Has Never Been Anyone Quite Like Him

One **sunday** I came in barely able to straighten up
Even with a cane and in terrible pain
Two days later the pain was gone and I could walk again

You give so much and expect so little
Even though my bones are brittle

You even gave me relief from Fibromyalgia when other
Doctors did not believe it was a real disease

In your words **"a piano 25% out of tune is still out of tune I
wish more could be done. I am not taking any more of your
money if I can't get you to that 100%"**

I believe in acupuncture more than a little. I believe in it a
lot. Especially when I lay on my favorite cot

I am trying to think of something bad to say,
But in your case I cannot

If this seems to be too good to be true,
It is because this testimonial is real. It has been real for me
for over 20 years

For All You Do

I was in your office today.
It struck me in an unusual way

The nurse was kind and didn't mind.
Showing me the people you are close to
And always on your mind

We are alike in many ways
We both have beautiful wives
And good looking sons

I have two sons and a beautiful daughter.
I think about them constantly as I am sure you do

You have quite a support group and I do too.
I know they are proud of what you do
As mine are of me and my artistic ability

I know I am feeling as well as can be expected.
I owe it to you

Thanks for being there, Dr. Wald
your grateful patient   Bob Purcell

Good Mechanics are hard to find

(Honest ones even harder)

He will find the answer to your car's performance

Problem that is bugging you

And if he is able to get it done cheaper

He will pass the savings on to you

He knows if you are unhappy in any way
You won't be back

But he wants you to stay

Good mechanics that are fair and true
Are hard to find

In Jim's case I know I found mine

I will keep sending him customers, my family included

Now that is a testimonial that is not diluted

Satisfied for 30+ years   R.M. Purcell

If He Fixed My Problem Omar
Can Fix Anybody's

Omar is a man at Dell the problems with your
Computer he can practically smell

He works hard at customer satisfaction as well

I can attest to his prowess and tell you he is the only
One that could fix my Dell

He recognized that my computer was not registered to
me so he fixed that for me

Now he said the drivers that were missing he could
load for me
I just had to sit back and watch him fix it remotely

Thanks Greg Milburn

The insurance agent that won't leave you poor
As a church mouse
He will even let you have money left over to buy a house

Don't be surprised if he offers you a deal
To insure all your cars and your house
He is real, he is an independent agent and
That gives him clout
To find a company with the best deal

You won't be as they say in the game "Insurance Poor"
You will have money left over and, you won't miss a meal

He is generally concerned for the people he can help
And if there is a claim he will settle it fast
You have only you to blame
If you don't sign up with him fast

So call him at 837-1078 don't wait
It could be the most rewarding thing you've done of late

Thanks Nancy

Nancy is the kindest nurse I know
I am happy to say so

She will help you get the care
You need when you need it.
Not just put you in a list like others I know

She does not put you ahead of anyone
She monitors what you need and the time that is needed to get it done

Her service to a patient comes first
You are not a number that gets lost on her desk

You are a person who just might need
To be served faster than the rest

A pain clinic is tough to manage; There must be someone to help the
Doctor decide who has a case that can wait. And those who cannot

If you are honest with her, Nancy can be honest with you and get you
The help you need because you need it

She does a good job of keeping patients happy
With an illness like mine I have known her as a

Receptionist, through her nursing education classes
And all the years after while she has been helping the masses

Dave the Tax Man

(can use the tune to Liberty Valance)

Well out of his house he built a
Business in this troubled world

A man, the kind of man who will do
Your taxes the best he can

He will find the deductions that you deserve
When you get your refund from the I R S

You'll be happy to see what they wrote
On the refund ch ...eck

He is the man who gets all your deductions
He sets up all your tax shelters

He is the best tax man you'll find
He even gives you peace of mind
He is the best of them all

Up Above Will Trim Your Tree

When you need, your trees trimmed
Just look for **Up Above** tree service

When you call they will do the rest
While you just rest

A job that you would have done
When you were young

Is better left to the professionals
Because they know the safe way to get it done

If you did it you would leave
A mess for weeks to come

Many thanks to Paul and Tim
For having, affordable rates again

Ode to Carlton Hall

It's easy to see why he is the
Best respiratory therapist of them all

He treats you the same way he would like to be treated
He doesn't get upset if you ask him to repeat it

The information he gives is as good as gold
Even if I am 60 years old

Carlton explains your problem and won't go on
Until he is sure you understand
Why you have the trouble that is at hand

Leaks around your mask are robbing you of quality sleep,
Because the air you should be getting is passing you by
Causing you to suffocate and panic. That's why

When I write about the truth, it's easy to see
How easy the words can come to me

My sleep is better now; I can rest like them all
Who have sought help from Carlton Hall

Thanks, R. M. Purcell